THE Cruise Planner

by Cathy Rogers

Published by JJ Moffs Independent Book Publisher 2019

JJMoffs Independent Book Publisher Ltd
Grove House Farm, Grovewood Road,
Misterton, Nottinghamshire DN10 4EF

Typeset by Anna Richards
Cover by The Brand Pharmacy

REWARD!

This book represents many hours spent planning my
perfect cruise!

If found please call me

....

THANK YOU!

Also by Cathy Rogers

The Confident portExplorer

WELCOME TO THE
CRUISE PLANNER AND JOURNAL!

Whilst this planner has been written using ideas discussed in my book, you don't have to have read The Confident portExplorer (or even have heard of it!), to be able to use it. You have space here to plan a two week cruise so there may be too much or too little for your exact plans... if necessary photocopy and stick more pages in or even cut some out! This is YOUR book now so don't be afraid to cross out or re-label any bits that don't apply to you.

There are FIVE sections:

Where, when, how - a place to record all the essentials as you book them and a memory jogger of things still to do.

Plotting and planning - worksheets for deciding how you want to spend your time ashore and who you will book excursions with.

Getting ready to go - our suggestions on what to take with you and packing lists for you to personalise.

On board and ashore - diary pages to record all your bookings and plans, with journal space to reflect on the day's memories.

Time to go home - a short section to gently ease you back to the real world!

I really hope you enjoy using the book and keep it for many years as a reference, and to remind you of a wonderful cruise. If you have any suggestions for future editions I would love to hear them - join our Facebook group talkExplore and let me know what you think.

Happy portExploring!   Cathy x

"Your reason and your passion are the rudder and the sails of your seafaring soul." -
Kahlil Gibran

CRUISE DETAILS

Cruiseline: _____

Ship: _____

From: _____

To: _____

Cruise reference number: _____

Number of nights abroad: _____

Dates of cruise: _____

Dates away from home: _____

Cabin number: _____ Deck: _____

Cruise loyalty scheme

Number: _____ Level: _____

Cruise company name: _____

Agent name: _____

Email: _____

Contact number: _____ Booking ref: _____

"The journey, not the arrival matters" - *T S Eliot*

BOOKING DETAILS

Details of 'perks' included in booking

OBC (onboard credit) _____

Drinks package (level) _____

Speciality dining package _____

WiFi package _____

Port parking _____

Chauffeur/transfers _____

Other _____

Bed configuration requested:

Double/twin/extra bunks

Dining option requested:

1st sitting/2nd sitting/anytime

Table size requested: _____

Any other requests made at time of booking:

_____

TRAVEL INSURANCE

Make sure this specifically includes cover for cruises and is valid for your entire time away

Cruise specific insurance through agent: _____

Policy purchased elsewhere: _____

Own annual policy: _____

Underwriting company: _____

Policy number: _____

Emergency contact number: _____

"Live life with no excuses, travel with no regret."
\- Oscar Wilde

HOME TO SHIP – TRAVEL PLANS

Self Drive to Port or Airport

If parking at port was included in your cruise booking, remember you need to confirm it and give your registration number

Date confirmed _____

Parking at Port/Airport

Date booked: _____ Company: _____

Contact number: _____

Email: _____

Cost: £ _____ Date paid: _____

Booking Confirmation

Documents received? _____ Printed? _____

Transfer to Port/Airport

Date booked: _____

If a transfer from home was included remember to confirm it.

Date confirmed: _____

Transfer by taxi/coach/limo/train/friend

Date booked: _____ Company: _____

Email: _____

Contact number: _____

Cost £ _____ Date paid: _____

Booking Confirmation

Documents received? _____ Printed? _____

7

"*I consider the sound of the sea to be part of my body*"
- *Derek Walcott*

Outward Flight

Date: _____ Fly-cruise/independent

Visa required? _____ Applied for? _____

Airline: _____ Flight no. _____

Airport: _____

Dep time: _____ Check-in time: _____

Arr. _____ Arr time: _____

Luggage allowance: _____

Airline Website/App Login

Username: _____ Password: _____

Advance Passenger Information (API) completed: _____

Seat numbers reserved: _____ Checked in: _____

Boarding pass printed: _____

Transfer from Airport to Port

Transfer by taxi/coach/limo/train/friend? Date booked: _____

Company: _____

Email: _____

Contact details: _____

Cost £ _____ Date paid: _____

Booking Confirmation

Documents received? _____ Printed? _____

"A man is never lost at sea." - Ernest Hemingway

HOTEL BOOKINGS

Pre-Cruise Hotels

1. Hotel name: _____

Contact number: _____

Address: _____

Email: _____

Date room booked/meals requested: _____

Booked through: _____

Confirmation printed? Y/N   TRANSFERS needed? Y/N

2. Hotel name: _____

Contact number: _____

Address: _____

Email: _____

Date room booked/meals requested: _____

Booked through: _____

Confirmation printed? Y/N   TRANSFERS needed? Y/N

Post-Cruise Hotels

Hotel name: _____

Contact number: _____

Address: _____

Email: _____

Date room booked/meals requested: _____

Booked through: _____

Confirmation printed? Y/N   TRANSFERS needed? Y/N

"Any damn fool can navigate the world sober. It takes a really good sailor to do it drunk." - Sir Francis Chichester

SHIP TO HOME – TRAVEL PLANS

Homeward Flight

Date: _____ Fly-cruise/independent

Airline: _____ Flight no. _____

Airport: _____

Dep time: _____ Check-in time: _____

Arr. _____ Arr time: _____

Luggage allowance: _____

Airline Website/App Login

Username: _____ Password: _____

Advance Passenger Information (API) completed: _____

Seat numbers reserved: _____ Checked in: _____

Boarding pass printed: _____

Transfer from Port/Airport to Home

Transfer by taxi/coach/limo/train/friend? Date booked: _____

Company: _____

Email: _____

Contact details: _____

Cost £ _____ Date paid: _____

Booking Confirmation

Documents received? _____ Printed? _____

"There is nothing more enticing, disenchanting and enslaving than the life at sea" -
Joseph Conrad

Cruiseline Cruise Personaliser

Login details

Username: _____

Password hint: _____

Check

Onboard credit allocated? _____

Dining allocation? _____

Room configuration? _____

Included drink packages visible? _____

Other requests noted? _____

How many formal/casual/gala evenings? _____

Pre-Order - if required or wait until on board

Drink packages? _____ Internet packages? _____

Photo packages? _____ Other? _____

Book - if required or wait until on board

Spa appointments? _____

Hair salon appointments? _____

Speciality restaurant bookings? _____

Ships tours/excursions?

1. _____

2. _____

3. _____

4. _____

"A ship in port is safe, but that's not what ships are built for"
- Grace Hopper

THE 'CRUISE ARC PLANNER'

I use the phrase 'cruise arc' to mean how to take an overall view of your cruise. It gives you a way to plot the content and feel of your trip. The arc planner is a useful tool that ensures you don't plan so many exciting days, one on top of another, that you finish the cruise exhausted! For that reason, I originally considered calling this section 'HOW NOT TO NEED A SECOND HOLIDAY'!

You will find the planner on the next two pages, and it will give you a place to record information from various sources. Use the data from the itinerary in your cruise line Cruise Personaliser as a starting point, adding both the day of the week and the actual date. This is a big help when planning and making bookings as it's useful to know what day you will be in port, so that you can check what is on in town and the local opening times.

You will find sunrise/set times at timeanddate.com – these are particularly useful if cruising slightly out of season, especially on a repositioning cruise where times in port can be reduced. You don't want to be organising a scenic drive back to the ship when it's dark!

Making a note of these and also the local currency (with a 'ballpark figure' exchange rate from xe.com) will help you as you make your plans. Once you have filled in both port days and days at sea, the chart will start to show the overall arc or shape of the cruise and help you to plan the pace of your cruise.

We have also added a couple of extra days onto the planner to allow for pre and post cruise stay planning, add more or delete as necessary!

Cx

Cruise Day #	Day of Week	Date	Port
1			
2			
3			
4			
5			
6			
7			
8			
9			
10			
11			
12			
13			
14			

Tender Port?	Arrive Port	Depart Port	Sunrise Time	Sunset Time	Local Currency	Cruise Day #
						1
						2
						3
						4
						5
						6
						7
						8
						9
						10
						11
						12
						13
						14

"The sea, once it casts its spell, holds one in its net of wonder forever" - Jacques Cousteau

On the following pages, you will see that you have one worksheet and one notes page for each of ten ports. This should cover most two week cruises. It may seem an unusual approach, but I am really passionate about encouraging you to make sure that you are doing what YOU (and your companions) want to do and these sheets will direct and inform your discussions. In particular, I want to encourage you to avoid getting sucked into booking a long day on a coach just because 'everyone' will be going to Florence!

Look at all your options before booking anything. Be particularly careful of the word 'FOR' - it means that you are not docking at that place but will be some distance away; use Google maps or similar to work out just how far and see how long a drive it will be. If you only have ten hours ashore, do you really want to spend four of them sitting on a coach?

Start by looking at the Ship's Tours in your Personaliser (there's much more about this in *The Confident portExplorer*). These are considered to be the main highlights of the area and can handle large groups of tourists. However, a little research will show many alternatives that you personally might find more appealing. It may be that they aren't mainstream enough for the ship's tours to take in, or possibly they are just too small to cope with a large influx of cruisers. However, they could be perfect for an independent visit.

Make this your own individual cruise experience. Take some time to decide what you really want from your cruise; do you want to squeeze the most out of every moment ashore, or do you want a laid back holiday with a bit of sightseeing? Culture or white-water rafting? Don't forget to look back at the Cruise Arc Planner and make sure that you don't overload yourself with ten-hour excursions at every port, on every day!

Be a smart portExplorer!!   C x

"Think it over, Think it under" - Winnie The Pooh

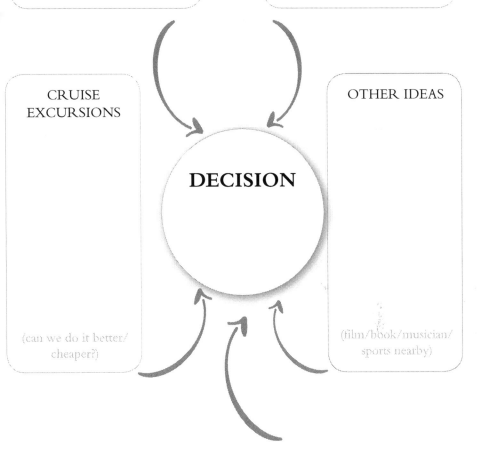

PORT

FOR?

HOW FAR AWAY IS IT?
(distance/time)

OTHER PLACES NEARBY

(look for places too small to take a
large cruise group)

CRUISE
EXCURSIONS

(can we do it better/
cheaper?)

DECISION

OTHER IDEAS

(film/book/musician/
sports nearby)

RECOMMENDATIONS (given by friends/family/online)

(Who did they use? Who did they contact? How can we do it?)

PLOTTING & PLANNING

"How inappropriate to call this planet Earth when it is clearly ocean." - Arthur C. Clarke

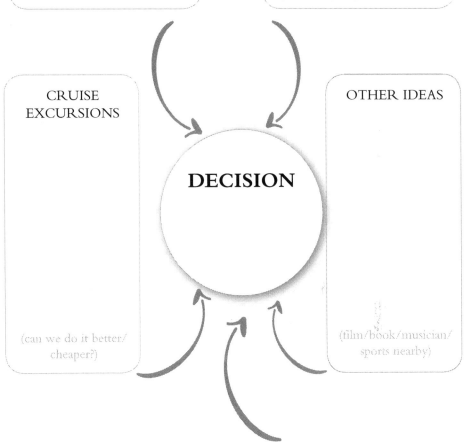

PORT

FOR?

HOW FAR AWAY IS IT?
(distance/time)

OTHER PLACES NEARBY

(look for places too small to take a
large cruise group)

CRUISE
EXCURSIONS

OTHER IDEAS

DECISION

(can we do it better/
cheaper?)

(film/book/musician/
sports nearby)

RECOMMENDATIONS (given by friends/family/online)

(Who did they use? Who did they contact? How can we do it?)

"For whatever we lose (like a you or a me), it's always our self we find in the sea." -
E.E. Cummings

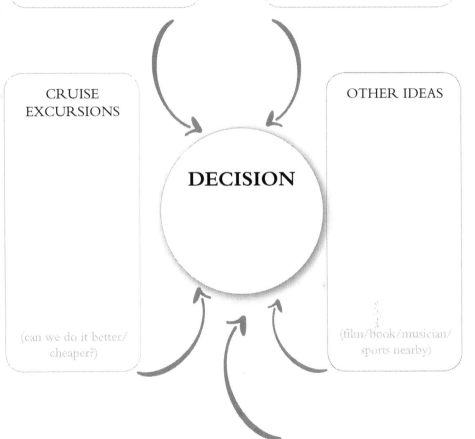

PORT

FOR?

HOW FAR AWAY IS IT?
(distance/time)

OTHER PLACES NEARBY

(look for places too small to take a large cruise group)

CRUISE EXCURSIONS

DECISION

OTHER IDEAS

(can we do it better/ cheaper?)

(film/book/musician/ sports nearby)

RECOMMENDATIONS (given by friends/family/online)

(Who did they use? Who did they contact? How can we do it?)

"The journey, not the arrival matters" - T S Eliot

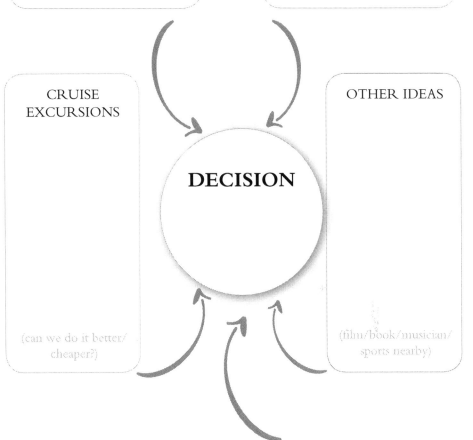

PORT

FOR?

HOW FAR AWAY IS IT?
(distance/time)

OTHER PLACES NEARBY

(look for places too small to take a large cruise group)

CRUISE
EXCURSIONS

OTHER IDEAS

DECISION

(can we do it better/cheaper?)

(film/book/musician/sports nearby)

RECOMMENDATIONS (given by friends/family/online)

(Who did they use? Who did they contact? How can we do it?)

"To the sea, to the sea! The white gulls are crying, the wind is blowing, and the white foam is flying." - J.R.R. Tolkien

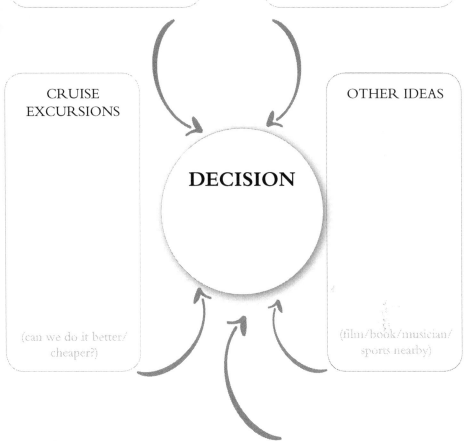

PORT

FOR?

HOW FAR AWAY IS IT?
(distance/time)

OTHER PLACES NEARBY

(look for places too small to take a
large cruise group)

CRUISE
EXCURSIONS

OTHER IDEAS

DECISION

(can we do it better/
cheaper?)

(film/book/musician/
sports nearby)

RECOMMENDATIONS (given by friends/family/online)

(Who did they use? Who did they contact? How can we do it?)

"Explore. Dream. Discover" - Mark Twain

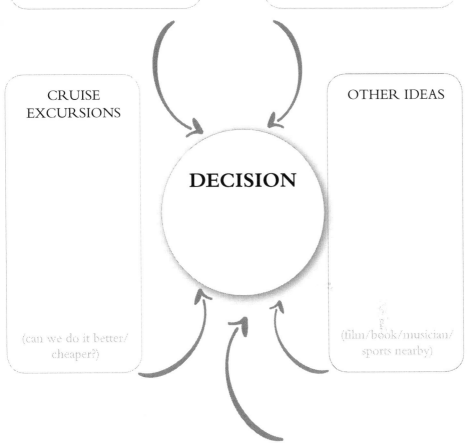

PORT

FOR?

HOW FAR AWAY IS IT?
(distance/time)

OTHER PLACES NEARBY

(look for places too small to take a large cruise group)

CRUISE EXCURSIONS

(can we do it better/ cheaper?)

DECISION

OTHER IDEAS

(film/book/musician/ sports nearby)

RECOMMENDATIONS (given by friends/family/online)

(Who did they use? Who did they contact? How can we do it?)

"There is nothing - absolutely nothing - half so much worth doing as simply messing about in boats" - Kenneth Grahame

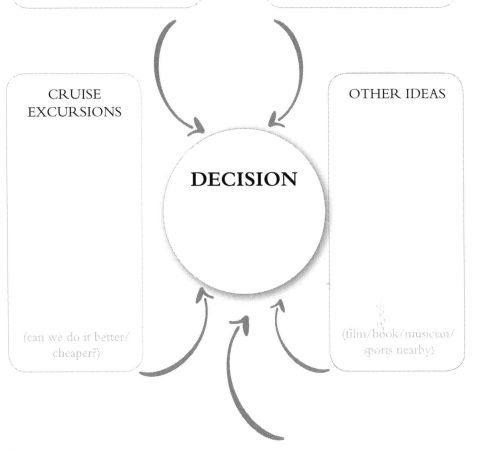

PORT

FOR?

HOW FAR AWAY IS IT?
(distance/time)

OTHER PLACES NEARBY

(look for places too small to take a large cruise group)

CRUISE EXCURSIONS

OTHER IDEAS

DECISION

(can we do it better/ cheaper?)

(film/book/musician/ sports nearby)

RECOMMENDATIONS (given by friends/family/online)

(Who did they use? Who did they contact? How can we do it?)

"It isn't that life ashore is distasteful to me. But life at sea is better."
- Sir Francis Drake

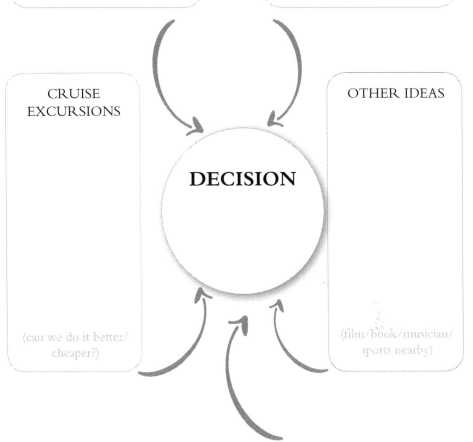

PORT

FOR?

HOW FAR AWAY IS IT?
(distance/time)

OTHER PLACES NEARBY

(look for places too small to take a large cruise group)

CRUISE EXCURSIONS

(can we do it better/cheaper?)

DECISION

OTHER IDEAS

(film/book/musician/sports nearby)

RECOMMENDATIONS (given by friends/family/online)

(Who did they use? Who did they contact? How can we do it?)

"You can put a Boat on a Ship but you cant put a Ship on a Boat"- Anon

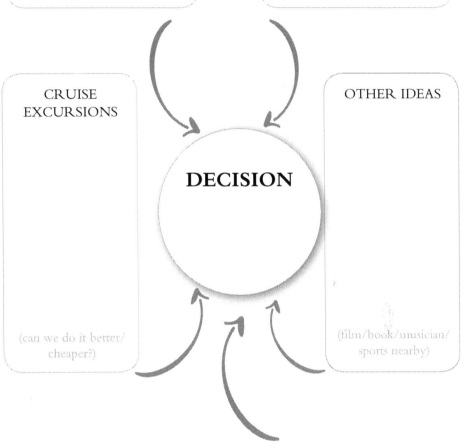

PORT

FOR?

HOW FAR AWAY IS IT?
(distance/time)

OTHER PLACES NEARBY

(look for places too small to take a
large cruise group)

CRUISE
EXCURSIONS

OTHER IDEAS

DECISION

(can we do it better/
cheaper?)

(film/book/musician/
sports nearby)

RECOMMENDATIONS (given by friends/family/online)

(Who did they use? Who did they contact? How can we do it?)

PLOTTING & PLANNING

"I wanted freedom, open air and adventure. I found it on the sea."
- Alaine Gerbault

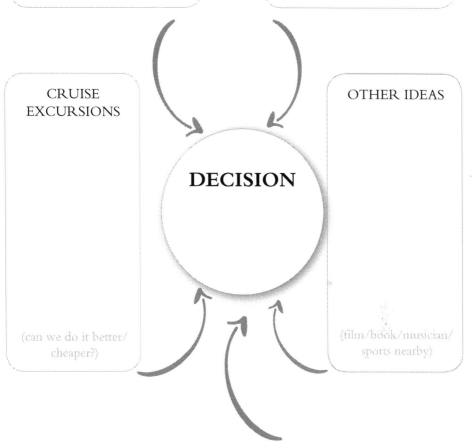

PORT

FOR?

HOW FAR AWAY IS IT?
(distance/time)

OTHER PLACES NEARBY

(look for places too small to take a large cruise group)

CRUISE EXCURSIONS

(can we do it better/ cheaper?)

DECISION

OTHER IDEAS

(film/book/musician/ sports nearby)

RECOMMENDATIONS (given by friends/family/online)

(Who did they use? Who did they contact? How can we do it?)

The 'Getting Ready to Go' next section is largely LISTS - I do love a good list!

These are mainly our suggestions of things for you to think about and I'm definitely not saying that you need to take all of it! Again, use this as you want, do whatever works for you and cross out/cut out/duplicate as you think best.

You will find lists of:

- Essential documents and other paperwork that you need to have with you
- Useful items to have on board
- Tech suggestions and reminders
- Toiletries and medicine cabinet
- Hot and cold weather cruising
- Cruising with kids (small/medium/large so pick and choose)
- Useful apps to download before you go
- Perfect hand baggage.

Have fun!!

C x

TOP 20 - DOCUMENTS
Delete if not relevant

Passport(s) *need to be valid six months after end of holiday* □

Visa(s) *if required* □

Car park confirmations, paperwork and contact details □

Flight e-tickets and boarding cards *pre and post cruise* □

Hotel confirmations and contact details *pre and post cruise* □

Cruise luggage labels *if affixing after flight (and stapler?)* □

Confirmation/check in documents □

Port agent contact details *for emergencies* □

Child travel consent *permission from any parent who is not travelling with you* □

Travel insurance details *and copy cover note* □

Booking confirmations *for all onshore excursions* □

Car hire confirmations □

Driving licence/International Driving Permit/DVLA certificate □

Doctor's prescription *for any prescription drugs you are taking with you* □

Doctor's letter/pre authorised drug listing for UAE *if needed* □

List of credit cards *and international customer assistance contact details* □

Local currency and currency cheat sheet as required □

Professional ID/membership cards/student cards *for discounts* □

Emergency contact phone list *with international codes* □

Photocopies of passports *(or copy as photo on phone)* □

TOP 20 PACKING - USEFUL ITEMS

Is it for you? ✓

Sticky 'Post-it' notes *reminders for you and messages for others* ☐

Champagne stopper *makes a 'welcome' bottle last up to 3 days apparently!* ☐

Small LED torch *no reason, but always useful!* ☐

Refillable water bottle ☐

Extendable mini clothes line *wet swim gear is too heavy for the shower one!* ☐

Notebook - or this planner! ☐

Battery operated nightlight *for bathroom* ☐

Highlighter pens for daily programme ☐

Corkscrew/bottle opener in checked luggage! ☐

Travel sewing kit and a couple of spare buttons ☐

Stain remover wipes ☐

Lingerie bags and own wash pods *or similar if launderette on board* ☐

Hanging shoe organiser *over back of wardrobe door gives extra storage* ☐

Tea bags/instant coffee/cordial *hot/cold water always available in buffet* ☐

Small supply snacks/breakfast bars etc. for days ashore ☐

Earplugs if you are a really light sleeper *see tech section* ☐

Spare glasses and sun glasses ☐

Magnets to fix notes etc to wall *magnetic hooks hold lightish items* ☐

Lanyard for cruise card? *personally I don't but many do…* ☐

Clock alarm - without auto update *NOT the one on your phone!* ☐

TOP 20 PACKING - USEFUL ITEMS

Is it packed? ✓

GETTING READY TO GO

TOP 20 PACKING - TECH SUGGESTIONS

Is it for you? ✓

Clock alarm - without auto update	*NOT the one on your phone! Again, yes! It's important!* ☐
SmartPhone	☐
Camera	☐
Ipad/tablet	☐
Kindle	☐
Speakers - bluetooth	☐
Power strip or extension cable *NOT surge protected - not allowed in ships*	☐
Multi USB travel charger	☐
Rechargeable power pack *with solar recharge?*	☐
Phone case with card pocket *will stop you deactivating your keycard!*	☐
RFID wallet - to protect cards in port. *Also passport cover?*	☐
SD card plugin for smartphone	*or external hard drive so that you upload pictures in case your camera is lost. Otherwise an SD card for every port.* ☐
Flexible tripod - Gorillapod style	☐
Go Pro - or other waterproof /action wearable camera	☐
Binoculars	☐
Wireless keyboard - for tablet/smartphone	☐
White noise machine or app *if light sleeper*	☐
Sleepbuds/noise cancelling earplugs *for light sleepers, BOSE are good*	☐
Digital luggage scale *if flying home*	☐
Selfie stick *or maybe not!*	☐

TOP 20 PACKING - TECH YOUR LIST

Is it packed? ✓

TOP 20 PACKING – OUR SUGGESTIONS FOR KIDS

Is it for you? ☑

BABY

Nappies/wet wipes/nappy sacks *not easily available or supplied on board* ☐

Washing up bowl *is a baby bath in shower/a mini pool beside your sun lounger* ☐

Small Tupperware/hand blender/sterilisation for bottles etc. ☐

Small travel 'stick on' sunshade for windows *both for days out & cabin* ☐

Baby carrier and compact stroller *for sleeping through restaurants & shows* ☐

BABY / TODDLER

Stain remover/own detergent & hand wash/washing line/pegs ☐

Small supply of familiar food and drink *formula, pouches, juice & biscuits* ☐

Thermometer/'Calpol' type meds *before calling the medical centre* ☐

Nightlight & battery operated candles *so you can relax in the evenings too* ☐

TODDLER

Swim nappies *although not all lines will allow* ☐

Small blow-up paddling pool *little ones can splash safely beside your lounger* ☐

Walking reins and compact stroller *for safety/sleeping in restaurants etc.* ☐

Small Tupperware/own bowl and cutlery ☐

TODDLER / KIDS

Small selection of new and familiar books, toys and games ☐

Own hand baggage *the Trunki range acts as a seat too* ☐

KIDS

Snacks/travel sweets/biscuits ☐

Download movies to tablet/DVD player and DVDs ☐

Walkie talkies/camera/binoculars ☐

Swim costumes/air bands/other floats *inflatables usually discouraged* ☐

Lanyard for cruise cards & name tags *for possessions/going to kid's club* ☐

TOP 20 PACKING - KIDS YOUR LIST

Is it packed? ✓

TOP 20 PACKING - CLOTHES OUR SUGGESTIONS

Is it for you? ✓

WOMEN Day shoes *comfortable trainers and/or walking shoes/flip flops for beach/pool/spa*	☐
Evening shoes *1 heeled and 1 flat pair - glitzy/jewelled that go with everything*	☐
Evening bag *1 (or 2) clutch purse - glitzy/jewelled that go with shoes*	☐
Evening shawl/scarf *as wrap for evenings and a coverup in churches/mosques*	☐
2/3 sets of trousers, capris and tops *that interchange for different looks*	☐
Dress or 2? *Simple/dressy/killer as you like, always OK with shoes/bag as above*	☐
Jewellery – LOTS *will give a variety of looks with above, take costume not real*	☐
Bikini/swimming costume *take 2 as not always easy to dry quickly in cabin*	☐
Cover up for above *functional or glamorous, your choice, to go with flip flops*	☐

WOMEN / MEN Bag that doubles as a pool bag/going ashore bag *or two separate ones*	☐
'Normal' going ashore clothes *for the season that the locals think it is!*	☐
Gym kit *leggings/top and jacket for gym/yoga/zumba/walks on deck and breakfast!*	☐
Day clothes - nothing dressy needed *shorts/trousers/t-shirts - all fine*	☐
Warm windproof jacket *for early morning sail-ins/sightings of whales/volcanos*	☐

MEN Long trousers/chinos for evenings *('dress shorts' are apparently also a thing?)*	☐
Buttoned shirts/polo shirts for evenings	☐
Jacket (and tie?) for 'smart' evenings and if cold	☐
Full James Bond kit *Tux/shirt bow tie combo (cuff links) - only if you want to!*	☐
Day shoes *comfortable trainers and/or walking shoes and sandals for beach/pool*	☐
Swimming trunks *2 unless quick drying, not always easy to dry in cabin*	☐

TOP 20 PACKING - CLOTHES YOUR LIST

Is it packed? ✓

TOP 20 PACKING - HOT OR COLD CRUISE OUR LIST

Is it for you? ☑

HOT

Insect repellent/sunscreen *you may need before you can buy* ☐

Beach shoes/hat *you can buy locally but why waste time?* ☐

Waterproof case for money and cards *then everyone can swim together* ☐

Beach bag *you'll get less hassle if you avoid using bags with cruise logos ashore* ☐

Snorkelling gear *will always be nicer than anything you hire. Prescription goggles?* ☐

Beach towels *make you much less obvious than using ships towels ashore* ☐

Towel pegs *stop your towels blowing away and show you which is your lounger!* ☐

Cooling gel/spray for feet, aftersun cream ☐

Hand held fan *battery operated or old style!* ☐

Something to mask unpleasant smells *menthol type sticks work well* ☐

COLD

Insulated mug *take a hot drink on deck for morning sail ins or whale watching* ☐

Hat and gloves *queuing for a tender can be bitterly cold in Norway, even in June!* ☐

Travel hot water bottle/bed socks *if you're a chilly mortal & feel cold in bed* ☐

Wind proof jacket *with a disposable rain poncho in the pocket, if not waterproof!* ☐

Emergency folded space blanket *you've worked out that I feel the cold now!* ☐

Gel hand warmers - ditto! ☐

Moisturiser and lip salve *cold is as bad as hot for skin!* ☐

Clothes that 'double duty' as layers *silk or merino vests and scarves/leggings* ☐

Waterproof shoes or waterproof spray *no-one wants wet feet* ☐

Roll of plastic bags *to protect cameras & phones and to put your wet gear in* ☐

TOP 20 PACKING - HOT OR COLD CRUISE YOUR LIST

Is it packed? ✓

TOP 20 PACKING – TOILETRIES OUR LIST

Is it for you? ✓

Body lotion *often supplied but you may prefer your own* ☐

Cleanser/toner ☐

Conditioner *often supplied but you may prefer your own* ☐

Contact lenses and solutions ☐

Deodorant ☐

Facial wipes, tissues/cotton buds ☐

Hairbrush/comb ☐

Hairdryer *supplied but you may prefer your own* ☐

Hairspray ☐

Hair straighteners/tongs – if used ☐

Lip balm ☐

Manicure kit *scissors, emery board, clippers etc.* ☐

Moisturiser/serum ☐

Nail varnish and remover ☐

Perfume/cologne ☐

Shaving kit *razor, blades, foam, cream etc.* ☐

Shower gel/soap *often supplied but you may prefer your own* ☐

Sunscreen ☐

Shampoo *often supplied but you may prefer your own* ☐

Toothbrush *and toothpaste/mouthwash/dental floss* ☐

TOP 20 PACKING - TOILETRIES YOUR LIST

Is it packed? ✓

TOP 20 PACKING - MEDICINIE CABINET OUR LIST

Is it for you? ✓

Travel first-aid kit *plasters, antiseptic wipes and ointment*	☐
Essential oils - tea tree, lavender, eucalyptus	☐
Sea sickness remedies *tablets, bands, ginger products*	☐
Aloe vera or other aftersun remedy	☐
Anti bacterial wipes	☐
Antihistamine tablets for allergic reactions	☐
Antihistamine or other insect bite cream	☐
Aspirin or similar	☐
Cold remedy	☐
Children's medicines - Calpol etc.	☐
Eye drops for dry/itchy eyes	☐
Ibroprufen tablets or gel	☐
Indigestion remedy or antacid tablets	☐
Immodium or other diarrhoea medicine	☐
Milk thistle *apparently helps liver function...*	☐
Paracetamol or similar	☐
Senna or other laxative	☐
Sinus medication	☐
Thermometer	☐
Vitamins - if taken	☐

TOP 20 PACKING - MEDICINE CABINET YOUR LIST

Is it packed? ✓

In our connected world where most people use a smartphone daily there are loads of handy, simple apps that can really make a difference to a cruise. Whether you want to check the weather, your spending or plan your wardrobe we have found some of the best FREE apps for you to download before you leave home. This is because internet onboard is a) expensive and b) slow! Have a look at our suggestions and, if you find something else that is helpful to have on board, then be sure to let us know - just make sure you can use the app without having to connect to the internet or it will drive you mad!

✓✗

USEFUL CRUISE APPS - DOWNLOAD BEFORE YOU GO!

- **BOATWATCH:** Lets you track your ship and its voyage, see nautical charts of the area you are in, identify ships and read information about them.
- **PREDICT WIND:** Accurate local marine forecasts of wind, rain, cloud, swell and temperature in map and table format. Can get quite addictive!
- **GOOGLE TRANSLATE:** Will translate spoken word and text in images instantly. Translates 59 languages offline - 103 online. Phrasebook function for saving translations of useful words.
- **DUOLINGO:** Great for learning language basics before you go. Has some functionality offline but needs to be online to progress through different levels.
- **WAYGO:** Translates pictograms in Chinese, Japanese and Korean offline using your phone's camera to instantly translate menus, information and signs into English.
- **STYLEBOOK:** Photograph your clothes (or download images from online shopping) to create a virtual wardrobe, keep a record of what you packed for each cruise and to try out different combinations of clothes and accessories.
- **GOOGLE MAPS:** Useful for both planning & when ashore. Gives real time GPS navigation with public transport & traffic info. Great for searching for alternative routes, it gives real journey times and distances between locations. Shows restaurants/shops/bars etc.

- **STAR WALK:** Brilliant stargazing app, shows planets and stars in real time as you turn your phone, augmented with graphics to show the constellations. Lots of other information too including an ISS lookout. Brilliant at sea away from light pollution.

- **FLIGHT RADAR:** Fun to see where the planes overhead are travelling to and from. Useful for tracking flights and checking up to date flight times.

- **ESPLORIO:** Battery efficient travel journal that records all the places you visit, maps your route with GPS and uploads any pictures you take into location based files once back online. Send photos home, direct from your phone, as personalised postcards.

- **MONZO:** Works with a commission free Monzo currency card to give you instant currency conversions and real time confirmation of transactions in your own currency. Has useful budget and bill splitting functions if travelling with other card holders.

- **PACK THE BAG:** If you prefer to keep your packing lists on your phone then this flexible app creates and stores your packing lists for every eventuality.

- **WHITE NOISE LITE:** Brilliant for any sort of sleep issues, this is particularly useful on a cruise if unusual noises disturb you easily. Nap function is great for dealing with jet lag.

APPS TO DOWNLOAD

Always download the specific app for your cruise line and/or ship. There are huge differences between different companies and these apps only work to their full capacity once you are onboard. Download before you go anyway so that you are all set up and ready to go. The exact functions will vary but normally include access to your itinerary, the daily schedule, weather forecasts, deck plans, restaurant menus, onboard account statements and links any bookings you've made. Sometimes you can use the app to message to others on board without charge. These apps normally run on the ship's free wi-fi. These apps are constantly being updated, so do check on your cruise personaliser for the latest editions and make sure to dowload the correct app for your specific ship.

This is the March 2019 list by Cruiseline:

Azamara 3DI (Azamara Club Cruises)

My Celebrity - Celebrity Cruises

Crystal Esprit/Media Player/PressReader/Preview/Crystal Cruises

Navigator - Disney Cruise Line

Holland America Line Navigator - HAL

MSC Cruises/MSC for Me/MSC Traveller - MSC Cruises

Cruise Norwegian/iConcierge - NCL

Princess@Sea - Princess Cruises

Royal Caribbean Guest App - RCI

Viking Voyager -Viking Ocean Cruises

THE PERFECT 'CARRY-ON' BAG

You will keep this with you until your room is ready, but if your luggage is delayed or even lost this may be all you have for a couple of days so it needs to contain some essentials. Use a wheeled cabin bag that will also double as an overnight bag on your last night.

• Your folder of **cruise documents**
• This **planner and pen** to fill in any forms
• **Luggage labels** and stapler/tag if not already on suitcases
• Your wallet/purse with **credit card** for onboard account
• A currency or **debit card**
• Any **local currency** you are taking
• **Smartphone**
• **Camera**
• Kindle/tablet/iPad/laptop and **chargers**
• Rechargeable **power pack**
• **Glasses** – prescription, reading and sunglasses
• All **essential medications** for cruise
• **Sun protection** – sunscreen/scarf/sunhat
• Basic **personal items** – hairbrush/comb/toothbrush
• **Change of clothes** – minimum change of underwear and a clean shirt/top
• **Swimwear** and flip-flops
• Valuable **jewellery** if taking
• **Makeup**
• If travelling with kids pack **books/cards/games** in case of delay

"Where there is sea, there are pirates" - Greek Proverb

This next section, Onboard and Ashore, is mainly a record of your cruise and also a journal of how you spend your days. You have somewhere to note details, both good and bad, about your cabin, dining experiences and the crew you come into daily contact with. It's worth doing as it's amazing how quickly you can forget which ship it was that had the amazing bathroom! There is also a little checklist and information about going ashore. Then a diary/journal page for each day so that you can fill in your reservations and plans etc., before you go. The space at the bottom is for you to reflect on the day, doodle or play noughts and crosses!

Whatever you like - your book, your choice... Cx

SHIP

Captain: _____

Other officers: _____

COMMENTS: _____

_____

CABIN

Number: _____ Deck: _____

Position: _____ Aft/mid/forward: _____

Steward's name: _____

COMMENTS: _____

_____

DINING EXPERIENCES

Dining room: _____ Sitting: 1st/2nd/anytime

Table companions: _____

Maitre'd: _____

Waiters: _____

Other restaurants & dining:

COMMENTS: _____

FAVOURITE BARS

Best barmen: _____

Favourite drink: _____

ENTERTAINMENT

Cruise director: _____

Best shows: _____

Other entertainers: _____

COMMENTS: _____

GOING ASHORE

There are some things that are sensible to take ashore whether you're going ashore with a ship's tour or exploring on your own. This is not solely in order to survive if you 'miss the boat' but also in the case of a local or medical emergency. I suggest you keep a small pouch packed with the last seven items on this Essentials list, update it daily with the first four items and drop it in into your zippable and secure bag or backpack at every port.

DAILY DISEMBARKATION CHECKLIST

CRUISE CARD: this is your ID and passport. You will not be allowed ashore without it!

SMARTPHONE: even if not intending to use. Useful as time stamped camera to document problems.

SHIP'S DAILY PROGRAMME: for the Port Agent's number in case of emergency, and also the definitive 'All Aboard' time.

TICKETS/CONFIRMATIONS: for this port instructions, contact details, portExplore cheat sheet, maps and guidebook for today's adventure!

ID/COPY OF PASSPORT: for emergencies, for ID to change money and to access any age related discounts.

POWER PACK: to maintain contact with ship/others in an emergency. Alternatively phone charger lead as a minimum.

CREDIT CARD: for emergencies even if not intending to use. Local currency or debit card/cash for exchange.

ESSENTIAL MEDICATION: Take a small amount with you. Lack of essential medication could make a bad situation worse.

MEDICATION LIST/PRESCRIPTION: Take your current medication list if taking tablets ashore, to prove they are prescribed for you.

DRIVING LICENCE/CAR HIRE CONFIRMATION:
plus International Driving Permit or DVLA check code as needed.

TRAVEL INSURANCE DETAILS: Policy number/contact numbers. Maybe as a photo on your phone.

ON BOARD & ASHORE

"It's a ship!!" - everyone

DAY 1	Embarking from
Day	Plans, bookings and reservations
Date	Daytime:
Tonight is	Evening:

SPACE FOR YOUR NOTES & THOUGHTS …

ON BOARD & ASHORE

| DAY 2 | at sea/ashore in |

DAY 3	at sea/ashore in

DAY 4	at sea/ashore in

DAY 5	at sea/ashore in

DAY 6	at sea/ashore in

DAY 7	at sea/ashore in

| DAY 8 | at sea/ashore in |

DAY 9	at sea/ashore in

DAY 10	at sea/ashore in

DAY 11	at sea/ashore in

DAY 12	at sea/ashore in

DAY 13	at sea/ashore in

DAY 12	Disembark in

"Man cannot discover new oceans unless he has the courage to lose sight of the shore" - Andre Gide

This final short section, Time to go Home, is mainly just a few thoughts on what you need to have with you as you leave the ship at the end your cruise. Also, it is somewhere to note details of any crew that you want to nominate for good service on your passenger satisfaction survey, as well as somewhere to note the contact details of new friends you want to stay in touch with. I've included some contact detail tear-out slips so you can give your details to others.

I hope you've found this planner useful and that you'll keep it as a memento of your cruise.

DISEMBARKATION

On your last evening on board you need to...

Put your main baggage out for collection *probably before you go down to dinner unless you are carrying it yourself.* ☐

Confirm or check-in for any onward flights *use luggage scales to check weight of bags for flight.* ☐

Check what time you should disembark *and make breakfast plans* ☐

Make any future cruise reservations *the office will not be open in the morning.* ☐

Check and agree your onboard account *and register a credit card to pay your onboard account automatically.* ☐

Collect your passports from the Purser *or have them delivered back to you.* ☐

Empty your safe. ☐

Leave out a complete outfit to wear in the morning *including shoes!* ☐

Leave chargers out for phone/tablet etc *ready to pack in hand baggage* ☐

HAND BAGGAGE – USE YOUR WHEELED CARRY ON BAG

Passports ☐

Smartphone/charger/powerbank ☐

Flight e-tickets and boarding cards – if needed ☐

Hotel confirmations and contact details – if needed ☐

Car park/transfer paperwork and contact details ☐

Travel insurance details and copy cover note ☐

Car hire paperwork – if needed ☐

Last night's clothes and night stuff ☐

This planner! ☐

Toiletries *don't forget if flying home that normal hand baggage rules will apply - sharp objects and liquids in particular* ☐

Travel stuff as required *boiled sweets/neck support/noise cancelling headphones/book/kindle etc* ☐

Space for items confiscated by cruise line ☐
which will be returned as you leave - alcohol/candles etc. (Leave space to repack in main baggage if flying home)

CREW to nominate for good service awards:

Title	Department

"Coming back to where you started is not the same as never leaving."
- Terry Pratchett

It's been great spending time
with you – let's keep in touch!

Name:

Email:

Phone:

Facebook:

It's been great spending time
with you – let's keep in touch!

Name:

Email:

Phone:

Facebook:

It's been great spending time
with you – let's keep in touch!

Name:

Email:

Phone:

Facebook:

It's been great spending time
with you – let's keep in touch!

Name:

Email:

Phone:

Facebook:

It's been great spending time
with you – let's keep in touch!

Name:

Email:

Phone:

Facebook:

It's been great spending time
with you – let's keep in touch!

Name:

Email:

Phone:

Facebook:

Printed in Great Britain
by Amazon

33879664R00052